A BOOK
LOVER'S
DIARY

A BOOK LOVER'S DIARY

The Reader's Companion

FIREFLY BOOKS

For my grandfather, Terence William Barclay

A Book Lover's Diary: The Reader's Companion
ISBN-10: 1-55209-015-9   ISBN-13: 978-1-55209-015-2

A FIREFLY BOOK

Published by Firefly Books Ltd., 66 Leek Crescent
Richmond Hill, Ontario, Canada L4B 1H1

Published in the U.S. by Firefly Books (U.S.) Inc.
P.O. Box 1338, Ellicott Station, Buffalo, New York 14205

Conceived and edited by Shelagh Wallace
Design and original illustrations by Scott McKowen

Acknowledgements
We wish to thank those publishers who have given their permission
to reproduce excerpts from works still in copyright. If anyone has been
unintentionally omitted, we offer our apologies and ask that you notify
the publisher so you may be included in future editions.

Excerpt from IF ON A WINTER'S NIGHT A TRAVELER by Italo Calvino,
copyright ©1981 by Harcourt Brace & Company, reprinted by permission
of the publisher. Reprinted with permission from *If on a Winter's Night a
Traveler* by Italo Calvino, published by Key Porter Books, Toronto,
Ontario. Copyright ©1979

From WORDSTRUCK by Robert MacNeil. Copyright ©1989 by Neely
Productions, Ltd. Used by permission of Viking Penguin, a division of
Penguin Books USA Inc.

Excerpt from *Modern First Editions: Their Value to Collectors* by Joseph Connolly,
copyright ©1987 Little Brown & Co. (UK).

Excerpt from Pete Hamill's "D'Artagnan on Ninth Street: A Brooklyn Boy at
the Library." Copyright ©1988 by The New York Times Company. Reprinted
by permission.

Excerpt from *Better Than Life*. Copyright © Daniel Pennac, 1992. English
translation copyright © David Homel, 1994. Reprinted by permission of
Coach House Press.

Quotations by Doris Lessing and Germaine Greer extracted from THE
PLEASURE OF READING Edited by Antonia Fraser. Copyright ©1992.
Reprinted by permission of Alfred A. Knopf Canada and Alfred A.
Knopf/Random House.

Excerpts from *The Reader's Quotation Book*, Pushcart Press, 1990.

Printed in Canada

n the shop window you have promptly identified the cover with the title you were looking for. Following this visual trail, you have forced your way through the shop past the thick barricade of Books You Haven't Read, *which were frowning at you from the tables and shelves, trying to cow you... And thus you pass the outer girdle of ramparts, but then you are attacked by the infantry of* Books That If You Had More Than One Life You Would Certainly Also Read But Unfortunately Your Days Are Numbered. *With a rapid maneuver you bypass them and move into the phalanxes of the* Books You Mean To Read But There Are Others You Must Read First, *the* Books Too Expensive Now And You'll Wait Till They're Remaindered, *the* Books ditto When They Come Out In Paperback, Books You Can Borrow From Somebody, Books That Everybody's Read So It's As If You Had Read Them, Too.

ITALO CALVINO, *IF ON A WINTER'S NIGHT A TRAVELER*

man should begin with his own times. He should become acquainted first of all with the world in which he is living and participating. He should not be afraid of reading too much or too little. He should take his reading as he does his food or his exercise. The good reader will gravitate to the good books. He will discover from his contemporaries what is inspiring or fecundating, or merely enjoyable, in past literature. He should have the pleasure of making these discoveries on his own, in his own way. What has worth, charm, beauty, wisdom, cannot be lost or forgotten. But things can lose all value, all charm and appeal, if one is dragged to them by the scalp. HENRY MILLER

BOOK
LISTS

he one way of tolerating existence is
to lose oneself in literature as in a
perpetual orgy.   GUSTAVE FLAUBERT

cannot live without books. THOMAS JEFFERSON

eople who don't read are brutes.
EUGENE IONESCO

_____

_____

_____

_____

_____

_____

_____

_____

_____

_____

_____

_____

_____

_____

_____

_____

_____

_____

_____

_____

_____

_____

_ay down a method also for your reading; let it be in a consistent and consecutive course, and not in that desultory and unmethodical manner, in which many people read scraps of different authors, upon different subjects. EARL OF CHESTERFIELD

riends can betray you but books are always loyal. WANG GHO ZHEN

ever judge a book by its movie.

ANONYMOUS

To compensate a little for the treachery and weakness of my memory, so extreme that it has happened to me more than once to pick up again... books which I have read carefully a few years before. I have adopted the habit for some time now of adding at the end of each book the time I finished reading it and the judgment I have derived of it as a whole, so that this may represent to me at least the sense and general idea I had conceived of the author in reading it.

MICHEL DE MONTAIGNE

RECORD
BOOK

TITLE

AUTHOR

PUBLISHER / PUB. DATE

LIBRARY / BOOKSTORE

DATE BORROWED / BOUGHT / READ

REVIEW / NOTES

RECOMMENDED BY / TO

TITLE

AUTHOR

PUBLISHER / PUB. DATE

LIBRARY / BOOKSTORE

DATE BORROWED / BOUGHT / READ

REVIEW / NOTES

RECOMMENDED BY / TO

TITLE

AUTHOR

PUBLISHER / PUB. DATE

LIBRARY / BOOKSTORE

DATE BORROWED / BOUGHT / READ

REVIEW / NOTES

RECOMMENDED BY / TO

TITLE

AUTHOR

PUBLISHER / PUB. DATE

LIBRARY / BOOKSTORE

DATE BORROWED / BOUGHT / READ

REVIEW / NOTES

RECOMMENDED BY / TO

TITLE

AUTHOR

PUBLISHER / PUB. DATE

LIBRARY / BOOKSTORE

DATE BORROWED / BOUGHT / READ

REVIEW / NOTES

RECOMMENDED BY / TO

TITLE

AUTHOR

PUBLISHER / PUB. DATE

LIBRARY / BOOKSTORE

DATE BORROWED / BOUGHT / READ

REVIEW / NOTES

RECOMMENDED BY / TO

TITLE

AUTHOR

PUBLISHER / PUB. DATE

LIBRARY / BOOKSTORE

DATE BORROWED / BOUGHT / READ

REVIEW / NOTES

RECOMMENDED BY / TO

TITLE

AUTHOR

PUBLISHER / PUB. DATE

LIBRARY / BOOKSTORE

DATE BORROWED / BOUGHT / READ

REVIEW / NOTES

RECOMMENDED BY / TO

TITLE

AUTHOR

PUBLISHER / PUB. DATE

LIBRARY / BOOKSTORE

DATE BORROWED / BOUGHT / READ

REVIEW / NOTES

RECOMMENDED BY / TO

TITLE

AUTHOR

PUBLISHER / PUB. DATE

LIBRARY / BOOKSTORE

DATE BORROWED / BOUGHT / READ

REVIEW / NOTES

RECOMMENDED BY / TO

TITLE

AUTHOR

PUBLISHER / PUB. DATE

LIBRARY / BOOKSTORE

DATE BORROWED / BOUGHT / READ

REVIEW / NOTES

RECOMMENDED BY / TO

TITLE

AUTHOR

PUBLISHER / PUB. DATE

LIBRARY / BOOKSTORE

DATE BORROWED / BOUGHT / READ

REVIEW / NOTES

RECOMMENDED BY / TO

TITLE

AUTHOR

PUBLISHER / PUB. DATE

LIBRARY / BOOKSTORE

DATE BORROWED / BOUGHT / READ

REVIEW / NOTES

RECOMMENDED BY / TO

TITLE

AUTHOR

PUBLISHER / PUB. DATE

LIBRARY / BOOKSTORE

DATE BORROWED / BOUGHT / READ

REVIEW / NOTES

RECOMMENDED BY / TO

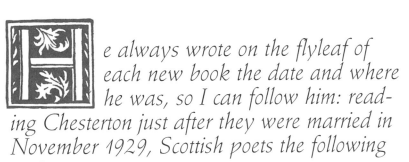

e always wrote on the flyleaf of each new book the date and where he was, so I can follow him: reading Chesterton just after they were married in November 1929, Scottish poets the following spring. ROBERT MACNEIL, *WORDSTRUCK: A MEMOIR*

TITLE

AUTHOR

PUBLISHER / PUB. DATE

LIBRARY / BOOKSTORE

DATE BORROWED / BOUGHT / READ

REVIEW / NOTES

RECOMMENDED BY / TO

TITLE

AUTHOR

PUBLISHER / PUB. DATE

LIBRARY / BOOKSTORE

DATE BORROWED / BOUGHT / READ

REVIEW / NOTES

RECOMMENDED BY / TO

TITLE

AUTHOR

PUBLISHER / PUB. DATE

LIBRARY / BOOKSTORE

DATE BORROWED / BOUGHT / READ

REVIEW / NOTES

RECOMMENDED BY / TO

TITLE

AUTHOR

PUBLISHER / PUB. DATE

LIBRARY / BOOKSTORE

DATE BORROWED / BOUGHT / READ

REVIEW / NOTES

RECOMMENDED BY / TO

TITLE

AUTHOR

PUBLISHER / PUB. DATE

LIBRARY / BOOKSTORE

DATE BORROWED / BOUGHT / READ

REVIEW / NOTES

RECOMMENDED BY / TO

TITLE

AUTHOR

PUBLISHER / PUB. DATE

LIBRARY / BOOKSTORE

DATE BORROWED / BOUGHT / READ

REVIEW / NOTES

RECOMMENDED BY / TO

TITLE

AUTHOR

PUBLISHER / PUB. DATE

LIBRARY / BOOKSTORE

DATE BORROWED / BOUGHT / READ

REVIEW / NOTES

RECOMMENDED BY / TO

TITLE

AUTHOR

PUBLISHER / PUB. DATE

LIBRARY / BOOKSTORE

DATE BORROWED / BOUGHT / READ

REVIEW / NOTES

RECOMMENDED BY / TO

TITLE

AUTHOR

PUBLISHER / PUB. DATE

LIBRARY / BOOKSTORE

DATE BORROWED / BOUGHT / READ

REVIEW / NOTES

RECOMMENDED BY / TO

TITLE

AUTHOR

PUBLISHER / PUB. DATE

LIBRARY / BOOKSTORE

DATE BORROWED / BOUGHT / READ

REVIEW / NOTES

RECOMMENDED BY / TO

TITLE

AUTHOR

PUBLISHER / PUB. DATE

LIBRARY / BOOKSTORE

DATE BORROWED / BOUGHT / READ

REVIEW / NOTES

RECOMMENDED BY / TO

TITLE

AUTHOR

PUBLISHER / PUB. DATE

LIBRARY / BOOKSTORE

DATE BORROWED / BOUGHT / READ

REVIEW / NOTES

RECOMMENDED BY / TO

TITLE

AUTHOR

PUBLISHER / PUB. DATE

LIBRARY / BOOKSTORE

DATE BORROWED / BOUGHT / READ

REVIEW / NOTES

RECOMMENDED BY / TO

TITLE

AUTHOR

PUBLISHER / PUB. DATE

LIBRARY / BOOKSTORE

DATE BORROWED / BOUGHT / READ

REVIEW / NOTES

RECOMMENDED BY / TO

TITLE

AUTHOR

PUBLISHER / PUB. DATE

LIBRARY / BOOKSTORE

DATE BORROWED / BOUGHT / READ

REVIEW / NOTES

RECOMMENDED BY / TO

TITLE

AUTHOR

PUBLISHER / PUB. DATE

LIBRARY / BOOKSTORE

DATE BORROWED / BOUGHT / READ

REVIEW / NOTES

RECOMMENDED BY / TO

TITLE

AUTHOR

PUBLISHER / PUB. DATE

LIBRARY / BOOKSTORE

DATE BORROWED / BOUGHT / READ

REVIEW / NOTES

RECOMMENDED BY / TO

TITLE

AUTHOR

PUBLISHER / PUB. DATE

LIBRARY / BOOKSTORE

DATE BORROWED / BOUGHT / READ

REVIEW / NOTES

RECOMMENDED BY / TO

TITLE

AUTHOR

PUBLISHER / PUB. DATE

LIBRARY / BOOKSTORE

DATE BORROWED / BOUGHT / READ

REVIEW / NOTES

RECOMMENDED BY / TO

TITLE

AUTHOR

PUBLISHER / PUB. DATE

LIBRARY / BOOKSTORE

DATE BORROWED / BOUGHT / READ

REVIEW / NOTES

RECOMMENDED BY / TO

 never travel without my diary.
One should always have something
sensational to read in the train.

OSCAR WILDE

TITLE

AUTHOR

PUBLISHER / PUB. DATE

LIBRARY / BOOKSTORE

DATE BORROWED / BOUGHT / READ

REVIEW / NOTES

RECOMMENDED BY / TO

TITLE

AUTHOR

PUBLISHER / PUB. DATE

LIBRARY / BOOKSTORE

DATE BORROWED / BOUGHT / READ

REVIEW / NOTES

RECOMMENDED BY / TO

TITLE

AUTHOR

PUBLISHER / PUB. DATE

LIBRARY / BOOKSTORE

DATE BORROWED / BOUGHT / READ

REVIEW / NOTES

RECOMMENDED BY / TO

TITLE

AUTHOR

PUBLISHER / PUB. DATE

LIBRARY / BOOKSTORE

DATE BORROWED / BOUGHT / READ

REVIEW / NOTES

RECOMMENDED BY / TO

TITLE

AUTHOR

PUBLISHER / PUB. DATE

LIBRARY / BOOKSTORE

DATE BORROWED / BOUGHT / READ

REVIEW / NOTES

RECOMMENDED BY / TO

TITLE

AUTHOR

PUBLISHER / PUB. DATE

LIBRARY / BOOKSTORE

DATE BORROWED / BOUGHT / READ

REVIEW / NOTES

RECOMMENDED BY / TO

TITLE

AUTHOR

PUBLISHER / PUB. DATE

LIBRARY / BOOKSTORE

DATE BORROWED / BOUGHT / READ

REVIEW / NOTES

RECOMMENDED BY / TO

TITLE

AUTHOR

PUBLISHER / PUB. DATE

LIBRARY / BOOKSTORE

DATE BORROWED / BOUGHT / READ

REVIEW / NOTES

RECOMMENDED BY / TO

TITLE

AUTHOR

PUBLISHER / PUB. DATE

LIBRARY / BOOKSTORE

DATE BORROWED / BOUGHT / READ

REVIEW / NOTES

RECOMMENDED BY / TO

TITLE

AUTHOR

PUBLISHER / PUB. DATE

LIBRARY / BOOKSTORE

DATE BORROWED / BOUGHT / READ

REVIEW / NOTES

RECOMMENDED BY / TO

TITLE

AUTHOR

PUBLISHER / PUB. DATE

LIBRARY / BOOKSTORE

DATE BORROWED / BOUGHT / READ

REVIEW / NOTES

RECOMMENDED BY / TO

TITLE

AUTHOR

PUBLISHER / PUB. DATE

LIBRARY / BOOKSTORE

DATE BORROWED / BOUGHT / READ

REVIEW / NOTES

RECOMMENDED BY / TO

TITLE

AUTHOR

PUBLISHER / PUB. DATE

LIBRARY / BOOKSTORE

DATE BORROWED / BOUGHT / READ

REVIEW / NOTES

RECOMMENDED BY / TO

TITLE

AUTHOR

PUBLISHER / PUB. DATE

LIBRARY / BOOKSTORE

DATE BORROWED / BOUGHT / READ

REVIEW / NOTES

RECOMMENDED BY / TO

TITLE

AUTHOR

PUBLISHER / PUB. DATE

LIBRARY / BOOKSTORE

DATE BORROWED / BOUGHT / READ

REVIEW / NOTES

RECOMMENDED BY / TO

TITLE

AUTHOR

PUBLISHER / PUB. DATE

LIBRARY / BOOKSTORE

DATE BORROWED / BOUGHT / READ

REVIEW / NOTES

RECOMMENDED BY / TO

TITLE

AUTHOR

PUBLISHER / PUB. DATE

LIBRARY / BOOKSTORE

DATE BORROWED / BOUGHT / READ

REVIEW / NOTES

RECOMMENDED BY / TO

TITLE

AUTHOR

PUBLISHER / PUB. DATE

LIBRARY / BOOKSTORE

DATE BORROWED / BOUGHT / READ

REVIEW / NOTES

RECOMMENDED BY / TO

AUTHOR	TITLE	DATE READ

You think your pains and your heartbreaks are unprecedented in the history of the world, but then you read. It was books that taught me that the things that tormented me were the very things that connected me with all the people who were alive, or who have ever been alive. JAMES BALDWIN

AUTHOR	TITLE	DATE READ

RECORD BOOK BY AUTHOR

AUTHOR	TITLE	DATE READ

 cLuhan Reads Books TORONTO GRAFFITI, 1966

AUTHOR	TITLE	DATE READ

AUTHOR	TITLE	DATE READ

AUTHOR	TITLE	DATE READ

AUTHOR	TITLE	DATE READ

AUTHOR	TITLE	DATE READ

AUTHOR	TITLE	DATE READ

AUTHOR	TITLE	DATE READ

he makers of literature are those who have seen and felt the miraculous interestingness of the universe. If you have formed...literary taste...your life will be one long ecstasy of denying that the world is a dull place. ARNOLD BENNETT, *LITERARY TASTE AND HOW TO FORM IT*

RECORD BOOK BY AUTHOR

AUTHOR	TITLE	DATE READ

AUTHOR	TITLE	DATE READ

AUTHOR	TITLE	DATE READ

he contents of someone's bookcase are part of his history, like an ancestral portrait. ANATOLE BROYARD

AUTHOR	TITLE	DATE READ

SUBJECT:

TITLE	AUTHOR	DATE READ

SUBJECT:

TITLE	AUTHOR	DATE READ

SUBJECT:

TITLE	AUTHOR	DATE READ

SUBJECT:

TITLE	AUTHOR	DATE READ

 eople say that life is the thing, but I prefer reading. LOGAN PEARSALL SMITH

SUBJECT:

TITLE	AUTHOR	DATE READ

SUBJECT:

TITLE	AUTHOR	DATE READ

SUBJECT:

TITLE	AUTHOR	DATE READ

t seems to me as natural and necessary to keep notes, however brief, of one's reading, as logs of voyages or photographs of one's travels. For memory, in most of us, is a liar with galloping consumption.

F. L. LUCAS

SUBJECT:

TITLE	AUTHOR	DATE READ

RECORD BOOK BY SUBJECT

SUBJECT:

TITLE	AUTHOR	DATE READ

SUBJECT:

TITLE	AUTHOR	DATE READ

SUBJECT:

TITLE	AUTHOR	DATE READ

SUBJECT:

TITLE	AUTHOR	DATE READ

book is meant not only to be read, but to haunt you, to importune you like a lover or a parent, to stick in your teeth like a piece of gristle. ANATOLE BROYARD

SUBJECT:

TITLE	AUTHOR	DATE READ

SUBJECT:

TITLE	AUTHOR	DATE READ

ry to avoid your house catching fire, as this does no good at all. And while your house is still intact, it is a sound idea to persuade all babies and animals to live in another one – and if you really value your books, only offer hospitality to illiterates who won't persist in bloody touching them all the time. Mind you, you will have to tolerate them telling you you could open a shop with all these books (people have suggested this to me – in the shop) and betting that you haven't read them all.

JOSEPH CONNOLLY, *MODERN FIRST EDITIONS*

BOOK
KEEPING

TITLE

AUTHOR

PUBLISHER / PUB. DATE

BOOKSTORE / DATE PURCHASED

NOTES

TITLE

AUTHOR

PUBLISHER / PUB. DATE

BOOKSTORE / DATE PURCHASED

NOTES

TITLE

AUTHOR

PUBLISHER / PUB. DATE

BOOKSTORE / DATE PURCHASED

NOTES

TITLE

AUTHOR

PUBLISHER / PUB. DATE

BOOKSTORE / DATE PURCHASED

NOTES

TITLE

AUTHOR

PUBLISHER / PUB. DATE

BOOKSTORE / DATE PURCHASED

NOTES

TITLE

AUTHOR

PUBLISHER / PUB. DATE

BOOKSTORE / DATE PURCHASED

NOTES

TITLE

AUTHOR

PUBLISHER / PUB. DATE

BOOKSTORE / DATE PURCHASED

NOTES

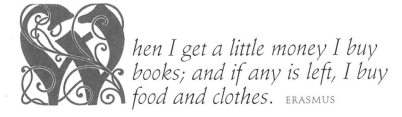

hen I get a little money I buy books; and if any is left, I buy food and clothes. ERASMUS

TITLE

AUTHOR

PUBLISHER / PUB. DATE

BOOKSTORE / DATE PURCHASED

NOTES

TITLE

AUTHOR

PUBLISHER / PUB. DATE

BOOKSTORE / DATE PURCHASED

NOTES

TITLE

AUTHOR

PUBLISHER / PUB. DATE

BOOKSTORE / DATE PURCHASED

NOTES

TITLE

AUTHOR

PUBLISHER / PUB. DATE

BOOKSTORE / DATE PURCHASED

NOTES

TITLE

AUTHOR

PUBLISHER / PUB. DATE

BOOKSTORE / DATE PURCHASED

NOTES

TITLE

AUTHOR

PUBLISHER / PUB. DATE

BOOKSTORE / DATE PURCHASED

NOTES

TITLE

AUTHOR

PUBLISHER / PUB. DATE

BOOKSTORE / DATE PURCHASED

NOTES

TITLE

AUTHOR

PUBLISHER / PUB. DATE

BOOKSTORE / DATE PURCHASED

NOTES

TITLE

AUTHOR

PUBLISHER / PUB. DATE

BOOKSTORE / DATE PURCHASED

NOTES

TITLE

AUTHOR

PUBLISHER / PUB. DATE

BOOKSTORE / DATE PURCHASED

NOTES

TITLE

AUTHOR

PUBLISHER / PUB. DATE

BOOKSTORE / DATE PURCHASED

NOTES

TITLE

AUTHOR

PUBLISHER / PUB. DATE

BOOKSTORE / DATE PURCHASED

NOTES

TITLE

AUTHOR

PUBLISHER / PUB. DATE

BOOKSTORE / DATE PURCHASED

NOTES

TITLE

AUTHOR

PUBLISHER / PUB. DATE

BOOKSTORE / DATE PURCHASED

NOTES

TITLE

AUTHOR

PUBLISHER / PUB. DATE

BOOKSTORE / DATE PURCHASED

NOTES

TITLE

AUTHOR

PUBLISHER / PUB. DATE

BOOKSTORE / DATE PURCHASED

NOTES

TITLE

AUTHOR

PUBLISHER / PUB. DATE

BOOKSTORE / DATE PURCHASED

NOTES

TITLE

AUTHOR

PUBLISHER / PUB. DATE

BOOKSTORE / DATE PURCHASED

NOTES

here are 10,000 books in my library, and it will keep growing until I die. This has exasperated my daughters, amused my friends and baffled my accountant. If I had not picked up this habit in the library long ago, I would have more money in the bank today; I would not be richer.

PETE HAMILL, "D'ARTAGNAN ON NINTH STREET:
A BROOKLYN BOY AT THE LIBRARY"

TITLE

AUTHOR

PUBLISHER / PUB. DATE

BOOKSTORE / DATE PURCHASED

NOTES

TITLE

AUTHOR

PUBLISHER / PUB. DATE

BOOKSTORE / DATE PURCHASED

NOTES

TITLE

AUTHOR

PUBLISHER / PUB. DATE

BOOKSTORE / DATE PURCHASED

NOTES

TITLE

AUTHOR

PUBLISHER / PUB. DATE

BOOKSTORE / DATE PURCHASED

NOTES

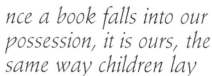nce a book falls into our possession, it is ours, the same way children lay their claim: 'That's my book.' As if it were organically part of them. That must be why we have so much trouble returning borrowed books. It's not exactly theft (of course not, we're not thieves, what are you implying¿); it's simply a slippage in ownership or, better still, a transfer of substance. That which belonged to someone else becomes mine when I look at it. And if I like what I read, naturally I'll have difficulty giving it back.

DANIEL PENNAC, *BETTER THAN LIFE*

SHARING
BOOKS

TITLE

AUTHOR

BORROWER

DATE BORROWED

DATE RETURNED

TITLE

AUTHOR

BORROWER

DATE BORROWED

DATE RETURNED

TITLE

AUTHOR

BORROWER

DATE BORROWED

DATE RETURNED

TITLE

AUTHOR

BORROWER

DATE BORROWED

DATE RETURNED

TITLE

AUTHOR

BORROWER

DATE BORROWED

DATE RETURNED

TITLE

AUTHOR

BORROWER

DATE BORROWED

DATE RETURNED

TITLE

AUTHOR

BORROWER

DATE BORROWED

DATE RETURNED

*mean your borrowers of books –
those mutilators of collections,
spoilers of the symmetry of shelves,
and creators of odd volumes.* CHARLES LAMB

TITLE

AUTHOR

BORROWER

DATE BORROWED

DATE RETURNED

TITLE

AUTHOR

BORROWER

DATE BORROWED

DATE RETURNED

TITLE

AUTHOR

BORROWER

DATE BORROWED

DATE RETURNED

TITLE

AUTHOR

BORROWER

DATE BORROWED

DATE RETURNED

TITLE

AUTHOR

BORROWER

DATE BORROWED

DATE RETURNED

TITLE

AUTHOR

BORROWER

DATE BORROWED

DATE RETURNED

TITLE

AUTHOR

BORROWER

DATE BORROWED

DATE RETURNED

TITLE

AUTHOR

BORROWER

DATE BORROWED

DATE RETURNED

TITLE

AUTHOR

LENDER

DATE BORROWED

DATE RETURNED

TITLE

AUTHOR

LENDER

DATE BORROWED

DATE RETURNED

TITLE

AUTHOR

LENDER

DATE BORROWED

DATE RETURNED

TITLE

AUTHOR

LENDER

DATE BORROWED

DATE RETURNED

TITLE

AUTHOR

LENDER

DATE BORROWED

DATE RETURNED

TITLE

AUTHOR

LENDER

DATE BORROWED

DATE RETURNED

TITLE

AUTHOR

LENDER

DATE BORROWED

DATE RETURNED

 verything comes to him who waits but a loaned book. FRANK MCKINNEY HUBBARD

TITLE

AUTHOR

LENDER

DATE BORROWED

DATE RETURNED

TITLE

AUTHOR

LENDER

DATE BORROWED

DATE RETURNED

TITLE

AUTHOR

LENDER

DATE BORROWED

DATE RETURNED

 *his Book Belongs to Norman Bethune and His Friends*
[BOOKPLATE, 1930S]

TITLE

AUTHOR

LENDER

DATE BORROWED

DATE RETURNED

TITLE

AUTHOR

LENDER

DATE BORROWED

DATE RETURNED

TITLE

AUTHOR

LENDER

DATE BORROWED

DATE RETURNED

TITLE

AUTHOR

LENDER

DATE BORROWED

DATE RETURNED

TITLE

AUTHOR

FROM

OCCASION

TITLE

AUTHOR

FROM

OCCASION

TITLE

AUTHOR

FROM

OCCASION

TITLE

AUTHOR

FROM

OCCASION

TITLE

AUTHOR

FROM

OCCASION

SHARING BOOKS BOOKS RECEIVED AS GIFTS

TITLE

AUTHOR

FROM

OCCASION

TITLE

AUTHOR

FROM

OCCASION

TITLE

AUTHOR

FROM

OCCASION

TITLE

AUTHOR

FROM

OCCASION

TITLE

AUTHOR

FROM

OCCASION

TITLE

AUTHOR

FROM

OCCASION

TITLE

AUTHOR

FROM

OCCASION

TITLE

AUTHOR

FROM

OCCASION

TITLE

AUTHOR

FROM

OCCASION

iterature illuminates life only for those to whom books are a necessity. Books are unconvertible assets, to be passed on only to those who possess them already.

ANTHONY POWELL

TITLE

AUTHOR

FROM

OCCASION

TITLE

AUTHOR

FROM

OCCASION

TITLE

AUTHOR

FROM

OCCASION

TITLE

AUTHOR

FROM

OCCASION

TITLE

AUTHOR

FROM

OCCASION

TITLE

AUTHOR

OCCASION

GIFT IDEAS

TITLE

AUTHOR

OCCASION

GIFT IDEAS

TITLE

AUTHOR

OCCASION

GIFT IDEAS

TITLE

AUTHOR

OCCASION

GIFT IDEAS

TITLE

AUTHOR

OCCASION

GIFT IDEAS

TITLE

AUTHOR

OCCASION

GIFT IDEAS

TITLE

AUTHOR

OCCASION

GIFT IDEAS

TITLE

AUTHOR

OCCASION

GIFT IDEAS

TITLE

AUTHOR

OCCASION

GIFT IDEAS

TITLE

AUTHOR

OCCASION

GIFT IDEAS

TITLE

AUTHOR

OCCASION

GIFT IDEAS

TITLE

AUTHOR

OCCASION

GIFT IDEAS

TITLE

AUTHOR

OCCASION

GIFT IDEAS

f you love the language, the greatest thing you can do to ensure its survival is not to complain about bad usage but to pass your enthusiasm to a child. Find a child and read to it often the things you admire, not being afraid to read the classics.

ROBERT MACNEIL, *WORDSTRUCK: A MEMOIR*

TITLE

AUTHOR

OCCASION

GIFT IDEAS

TITLE

AUTHOR

OCCASION

GIFT IDEAS

TITLE

AUTHOR

OCCASION

GIFT IDEAS

TITLE

AUTHOR

OCCASION

GIFT IDEAS

TITLE

AUTHOR

OCCASION

GIFT IDEAS

SHARING BOOKS BOOKS GIVEN AS GIFTS

GIFT FOR

OCCASION

TITLE

AUTHOR

GIFT FOR

OCCASION

TITLE

AUTHOR

GIFT FOR

OCCASION

TITLE

AUTHOR

GIFT FOR

OCCASION

TITLE

AUTHOR

GIFT FOR

OCCASION

TITLE

AUTHOR

GIFT FOR

OCCASION

TITLE

AUTHOR

GIFT FOR

OCCASION

TITLE

AUTHOR

GIFT FOR

OCCASION

TITLE

AUTHOR

GIFT FOR

OCCASION

TITLE

AUTHOR

GIFT FOR

OCCASION

TITLE

AUTHOR

GIFT FOR

OCCASION

TITLE

AUTHOR

GIFT FOR

OCCASION

TITLE

AUTHOR

GIFT FOR

OCCASION

TITLE

AUTHOR

GIFT FOR

OCCASION

TITLE

AUTHOR

e believe in books. Somehow we want to make childhood better, and we believe that a book given at the right moment can work magic in a child's life.

ANN SCHLEE

GIFT FOR

OCCASION

TITLE

AUTHOR

GIFT FOR

OCCASION

TITLE

AUTHOR

GIFT FOR

OCCASION

TITLE

AUTHOR

GIFT FOR

OCCASION

TITLE

AUTHOR

GIFT FOR

OCCASION

TITLE

AUTHOR

eading is a privileged pleasure because each of us enjoys it, quite complexly, in ways not replicable by anyone else. But there is enough structural common ground in the text itself so that we can talk to each other, even sometimes persuade each other, about what we read: and that many-voiced conversation, with which, thankfully, we shall never have done, is one of the most gratifying responses to literary creation, second only to reading itself. ROBERT ALTER

TALKING
ABOUT
BOOKS

NAME	ADDRESS	PHONE

MEETING DATE	TITLE	AUTHOR

DATE / PLACE / TIME

TITLE

AUTHOR

MEMBERS

NOTES

hat can we see, read, acquire, but ourselves. Take the book, my friend, and read your eyes out, you will never find there what I find. RALPH WALDO EMERSON

TALKING ABOUT BOOKS MEETING NOTES

DATE/PLACE/TIME

TITLE

AUTHOR

MEMBERS

NOTES

DATE / PLACE / TIME

TITLE

AUTHOR

MEMBERS

NOTES

DATE/PLACE/TIME

TITLE

AUTHOR

MEMBERS

NOTES

We have our responsibilities as readers and even our importance. The standards we raise and the judgments we pass steal in the air and become part of the atmosphere which writers breathe as they work. An influence is created which tells upon them even if it never finds its way into print.

VIRGINIA WOOLF

DATE / PLACE / TIME

TITLE

AUTHOR

MEMBERS

NOTES

DATE / PLACE / TIME

TITLE

AUTHOR

MEMBERS

NOTES

DATE / PLACE / TIME

TITLE

AUTHOR

MEMBERS

NOTES

DATE/PLACE/TIME

TITLE

AUTHOR

MEMBERS

NOTES

DATE / PLACE / TIME

TITLE

AUTHOR

MEMBERS

NOTES

DATE / PLACE / TIME

TITLE

AUTHOR

MEMBERS

NOTES

n the beginning the word was with God; all explanations, physical and moral, rested on the divine. And now for storytellers, even though those patterns of explanation are strictly human, the word has not lost a superhuman power to connect young and old, writer and reader; to connect us with each other and with the causes and consequences of what we do. JILL PATON WALSH

DATE/PLACE/TIME

TITLE

AUTHOR

MEMBERS

NOTES

TALKING ABOUT BOOKS MEETING NOTES

DATE/PLACE/TIME

TITLE

AUTHOR

MEMBERS

NOTES

loved [fairy stories] so, and my mother weighed down by grief had given up telling me them. At Nohant I found Mmes. d'Ardnoy's and Perrault's tales in old editions which became my chief joy for five or six years...I've never read them since, but I could tell each tale straight through, and I don't think anything in all one's intellectual life can be compared to these delights of the imagination. GEORGE SAND

BOOKS TO REMEMBER

IF I WERE STRANDED ON A DESERT ISLAND, I WOULD WANT TO HAVE THESE BOOKS WITH ME

IF I WERE STRANDED ON A DESERT ISLAND, I WOULD WANT TO HAVE THESE BOOKS WITH ME

ooks are for writing – not for reading. On a desert island, I should require the following: A manual on how to build a seaworthy boat; preferably by the gentleman who wrote Kon-Tiki. A manual on how to navigate a small craft in high seas: preferably by Mr Chichester. A handbook on how to attract the attention of rescue teams. A cook book containing recipes requiring no food and no stove, by Mrs Cradock. A tailoring manual demonstrating the way to make clothes from palm leaves, preferably by Mr Cardin. A long playing record saying, 'Help'. QUENTIN CRISP

BOOKS TO REMEMBER

I MUST REMEMBER TO READ THESE BOOKS AGAIN

I MUST REMEMBER TO READ THESE BOOKS AGAIN

n unliterary man may be defined as one who reads books once only. There is hope for a man who has never read Malory or Boswell or Tristram Shandy _or Shakespeare's_ Sonnets: _but what can you do with a man who says he 'has read' them, meaning he has read them once, and thinks that settles the matter._ C.S. LEWIS

BOOKS TO REMEMBER

WHEN I WAS A CHILD, MY FAVORITE BOOKS WERE

WHEN I WAS A CHILD, MY FAVORITE BOOKS WERE

eading was my first solitary vice (and led to all the others). I read while I ate, I read in the loo, I read in the bath. When I was supposed to be sleeping, I was reading. GERMAINE GREER

o book is worth anything which is not worth much; nor is it serviceable until it has been read, and re-read, and loved, and loved again; and marked, so that you can refer to the passages you want in it, as a soldier can seize the weapon he needs in an armory; or a housewife bring the spice she needs from her store. JOHN RUSKIN

BOOK
PASSAGES

BOOK PASSAGES

public library is the most democratic thing in the world. What can be found there has undone dictators and tyrants: demagogues can persecute writers and tell them what to write as much as they like, but they cannot vanish what has been written in the past, though they try often enough...People who love literature have at least part of their minds immune from indoctrination. If you read, you can learn to think for yourself. DORIS LESSING

ADDRESS
BOOK

NAME

ADDRESS

PHONE

NOTES

NAME

ADDRESS

PHONE

NOTES

NAME

ADDRESS

PHONE

NOTES

NAME

ADDRESS

PHONE

NOTES

NAME

ADDRESS

PHONE

NOTES